beating depression

HERE ARE SOME CLUES THAT IT MAY BE MORE THAN THE BLUES.

Do you:

1 find activities you usually enjoy to be less satisfying?

2 have overwhelming feelings of guilt, shame, hopelessness?

3 feel sad all the time and find yourself crying for no reason?

4 feel lonely and isolated, even from those you love?

5 have trouble focusing or sleeping due to your mood?

If you answered "yes" to any of these questions, you may be experiencing symptoms of depression. You should consider seeking guidance from a counselor or mental health professional, especially if your symptoms have been present for more than a few days. No one should have to face depression alone!

In memoriam: Fern Huebl and Caren Tropper

Photographs, 2007: age fotostock/Bartomeu Amengual/Pixtal:
80 bottom; Alamy Images/Phototake, Inc.: 41; AP/Wide World
Photos/Alan Levine/Casa Grande Dispatch: 81 bottom: Corbis
Images: 83 (Ajax/zefa), 24 (Susanne Borges/A.B./zefa), 87
(Robert Essel NYC), 13 (Estelle Klawitter/zefa), 96 (Tom &
Dee Ann McCarthy), 26 (Gabe Palmer), 42 right (Royalty-
Free), 6, 52, 93 (Larry Williams/zefa), 68 top (Michael S.
Yamashita); Getty Images: 5 top, 69 top (Tony Anderson), 39
(Bruce Ayres), 44 (Richard Cooke), 80 top (Zigy Kaluzny), 100
(Michael Kelley), 4, 14 (Richard Laird), 8 (Clarissa Leahy),
79 top (Lisa Petkau), 68 bottom (Russell Sadur); Jupiter-
Images: 2, 42 left (Bananstock), 36, 95 (Creatas), 56 (Alvia
Upitis); Monty Stilson: cover; PhotoEdit: 69 bottom (Michael D.
Bridwell), 5 bottom, 102 (Cleve Bryant), 92 (Felicia Martinez),
79 bottom (Michael Newman), 74, 75 (Jonathan A. Nourok),
91 (Rudi Von Briel); Superstock, Inc./age fotostock: 29, 62, 85:
The Image Works: 42 center (Bob Daemmrich), 90 (Richard
Lord); VEER: 20, 70, 94 (Ciaran Griffin/Stockbyte), 81 top
(Image Source).

Cover design: Marie O'Neill
Book production: The Design Lab

Library of Congress Cataloging-in-Publication Data
Zucker, Faye.
  Beating depression : teens find light at the end of the tunnel /
  by Faye Zucker & Joan E. Huebl.
     p. cm. — (Choices)
  Includes bibliographical references and index.
  ISBN-13: 978-0-531-12462-8 (lib. bdg) 978-0-531-17729-7 (pbk)
  ISBN-10: 0-531-12462-2 (lib. bdg) 0-531-17729-7 (pbk)
  1. Depression in adolescence—Popular works. 2. Depression in ado-
lescence—Treatment—Popular works. 3. Teenagers—Mental health. I.
Huebl, Joan E. II. Title. III. Series: Choices (Scholastic Inc.)
  RJ506.D4.Z83 2007
  618.92'8527—dc22   2006006779

2 3 4 5 6 7 8 9 10 R 16 15 14 13 12 11 10 09 08 07

■ SCHOLASTIC
CHOICES

Teens find
light at
the end of
the tunnel

beating
depression

Faye Zucker and Joan E. Huebl, PsyD

Franklin Watts®

A DIVISION OF SCHOLASTIC INC.
NEW YORK • TORONTO • LONDON • AUCKLAND • SYDNEY
MEXICO CITY • NEW DELHI • HONG KONG
DANBURY, CONNECTICUT

table of contents

chapter one

6 What Is Depression?

Depression is a complicated illness. Forget the myths and find out more about the realities.

1

chapter two

20 The Signs and Symptoms

How do you know if it's really depression? Learn what depression looks and feels like.

2

chapter three

36 Time Out for Science

It's not just blue moods, gray days, and low energy. It's about the genes, neurotransmitters, hormones, and hardwiring inside you.

3

chapter four

52 Getting Help

There is light at the end of the depression tunnel,
and science is discovering new treatments every day.

chapter five

70 Finding the Right Treatment

There are no guarantees, but a happier tomorrow is
possible with the right treatment and support.

MORE INFORMATION

104 **Glossary;** 106 **Further Resources;**
108 **Index;** 112 **About the Authors**

what is depression?

what is depression?

"WHAT'S WRONG WITH ME?"

Shannon's Story

Shannon, 18, was a bright and energetic student. But then a dark cloud came over her world.

Sophomore year in my Massachusetts high school was tough. I took a bunch of accelerated classes. I battled to stay on the ski team. And my math teacher had it in for me. All my papers came back covered in red ink. Then things got worse. I broke up with my boyfriend. We had gone out for a year. And he was the one person who understood me.

"When the morning came, I dreaded going to school."

So, yeah, you could say I was miserable. It's natural to be sad when you have a breakup. And I've always been a moody kid. I tend to see the glass as half empty. Feeling blue was nothing new to me. But this was different. I was so down. Weeks went by, and I couldn't get over it. I sat in the dark in my room. All of a sudden, I'd feel like crying. And then I couldn't stop sobbing. I wasn't sleeping or eating. I'd toss in bed at night. When the morning came, I dreaded going to school.

Schoolwork began to scare the daylights out of me. It wasn't hard. I could do it. After all, I was an A-student. But my backpack stayed in the corner of my room. I'd sit on my bed and look at it. Just the thought of pulling my homework out of that bag made me shake and panic. I even hyperventilated.

What's wrong with me? I thought. Why can't I snap out of this? My mom asked me if I wanted to see somebody. Like a shrink. But that was too weird. What was I going to tell them? "I broke up with my boyfriend, and now I'm falling to pieces?" No thanks.

Then I hit rock bottom.

My mom woke me for school one morning. I couldn't get out of bed. I wasn't tired or sick. But I couldn't get out of bed. It was like there was this giant weight on me. Even as I pulled myself to the floor, I felt so heavy. My legs wouldn't work. My mom told me to hurry or I'd be late. But I couldn't get dressed. I couldn't leave the house. The thought of stepping outside made me panic.

I didn't go to school that day. Or the next. Or the next. In fact, I didn't leave the house for a week. I sat on the couch, watching cartoons on TV. It took a major effort just to get in the car so my mom could drive me to Wendy's. We pulled up to the drive-thru window. I remember looking over at my mom in the driver's seat. I hadn't spoken in days. But I whispered, "Mom, I think I need some help."

"Mom, I think I need some help."

The Truth About Depression

There's no escaping it. Sometime, somewhere, you are going to get a bad case of the blues. You'll flunk a test at school. You'll break up with your one-and-only. Or your parents just won't get off your back. Teen life can be turbulent. It's bound to get you down now and then. But does that mean you're depressed?

Not necessarily. True depression is hard to spot and tricky to treat. But it's more than just feeling down in the dumps. Clinical depression is a serious illness that can affect anybody—even teenagers. It can impact your thoughts, feelings, behavior, and overall health. It can be caused by the chemicals in your brain, you can inherit it through your genes, or it can suddenly overtake you for seemingly no reason at all. "Depression is a complex illness," says Dr. David Fassler, a depression expert and a professor of psychiatry at the University of Vermont. "It's an oversimplification to say it's only caused by chemicals. Or to say that it's just being sad. There's a lot we don't know about it."

One in every ten teens suffers from clinical depression, according to the Center for Mental Health Services. It affects about 2.5 million people under the age of 18 in the United States alone. But it's not easy to spot. The signs and symptoms

the
warning signs
OF CLINICAL DEPRESSION

Experts generally agree on two big warning signs:

1 **Duration of symptoms**

2 **Intensity of symptoms**

of depression are numerous and can often be mistaken for a simple case of being a teen. Some depression signs include: feeling so low that nothing interests you; always being tired; and unreasonably dark feelings. On their own, they can simply mean you're having a bad day.

So how do you know if you're clinically depressed? Experts generally agree on two big warning signs: The *duration* of the symptoms—that's how long they last—and their *intensity*—that's how strong they are. If you're feeling overwhelmingly sad for a long period of time—more than two weeks—you might be depressed. If these feelings are interfering with your life—if you can't do your schoolwork or be with your friends or enjoy anything—you may have a problem.

Why Do People Get Depressed?

There's no single cause of depression. Many factors play a role—like your genes, your environment, and the way your brain works. But that doesn't tell the whole story. Some people have the right combination of conditions to get depressed—and never actually develop the condition. Others seem to get depressed for no reason at all. Still, experts say that most cases occur due to a combination of these factors:

Genetics: Depression can run in your family. You can inherit a combination of genes from your parents that may make you more likely to be depressed.

Brain chemistry:
There are chemicals in your brain called neurotransmitters. They send messages between the nerve cells of your brain. And they regulate your moods. When they're not working right—or you don't have enough of them—you can develop depression.

Sad events: Hard times in your life—everything from the death of a loved one to a breakup to flunking a test—can open the door to developing depression.

Family life: A negative, stressful, and unhappy family atmosphere can lead to depression.

Social conditions: Poverty, homelessness, and physical or emotional abuse can make it more likely for people to become depressed.

Substance abuse: Alcohol and drug use can cause chemical changes in the brain that affect mood and can lead to depression.

Who Gets
DEPRESSION?

More Americans suffer from depression than from AIDS, cancer, and heart failure combined. In the United States:

- **One in ten teenagers experiences major depression every year.**
- **One in ten people will experience depression at some point in life.**

10%
DEPRESSED

90%
NOT DEPRESSED

Not Depressed

Depressed

Source: U.S. Department of Health and Human Services. "Depression among Adolescents," *National Survey on Drug Use and Health*, 2005.

Age and Depression

People say the teen years can be rough, and the statistics prove it. The risk of depression increases drastically between the ages of 12 and 17. In 2005, an estimated 9 percent of adolescents—or 2.2 million kids—experienced major depression. Less than half received treatment. The 16- and 17-year-olds had it the hardest. Their rate of depression was 30 percent higher than that of other adolescents.

DEPRESSED

5.4%
12–13 year olds

9.2%
14–15 year olds

12.3%
16–17 year olds

Teens At Risk

As teenagers get older, their risk of experiencing depression increases.

Sources: U.S. Department of Health and Human Services. "Depression among Adolescents," *National Survey on Drug Use and Health*, 2005.

Gender and Depression

Up to the age of 13 or 14, boys and girls have roughly the same rates of depression. But when girls begin having periods, their risk for depression increases.

If all age groups between 12 and 17 are combined, about 5 percent of boys and an astonishing 13 percent of girls struggle with depression. This gender gap for depression continues throughout life. In 2004, 5.6 percent of men ages 18 and older and 10 percent of women reported experiencing at least one major episode of depression.

TYPES
of Depression

For some people, depression can be extremely intense—but it can go away quickly. Others feel a less severe depression, but the dark moods linger at a low level for years. In both cases the person is suffering from depression. Not all depressions are alike. **Experts generally divide depression into these categories:**

1 **Major depression** A severe form of depression that lasts longer than two weeks and requires treatment.

2 **Dysthymia** A longer-lasting but milder form of depression

3 **Reactive depression (or adjustment disorder)** A depressive reaction to a specific life event—like a death or a divorce. When your adjustment takes longer than normal, is more severe than expected, and interferes with your daily life, it is a depressive reaction.

4 **Seasonal Affective Disorder** A form of depression that strikes in winter when the daylight hours are shortened. Some people are highly sensitive to the seasonal change and can experience a very real form of depression.

5 **Bipolar disorder (or manic-depressive illness)** A serious type of depression characterized by wild mood swings (see "Bipolar Disorder" on page 44).

depression

can come in different shapes.
The most common ones are:

	MAJOR DEPRESSION	DYSTHYMIA	REACTIVE DEPRESSION
DEFINITION	extremely serious, long-lasting, and disabling depression	milder form of depression over a longer period of time	severe depression following a loss, trauma, or major life change
SYMPTOMS	includes sadness, fatigue, difficulty concentrating, overwhelming negative feelings or thoughts, changes in appetite or sleep	goes on for months or even years, marked by an inability to enjoy life, with possible periods of major depression	similar to major depression
TREATMENT	requires immediate treatment, usually including psychotherapy in combination with medication	though mild, treatment is still recommended and can include psychotherapy and/or medication	usually clears up following a period of adjusting to the change and counseling or therapy

SEASONAL AFFECTIVE DISORDER (SAD)	DEPRESSION AS PART OF ANOTHER ILLNESS
depression that occurs during certain parts of the year (worst months are autumn and winter; best are in spring and summer)	depression caused by a physical illness, such as Parkinson's disease or epilepsy
includes fatigue, increased appetite, irritability, or other depression symptoms during the winter months	similar symptoms to major depression, but accompanying the symptoms of another illness
often phototherapy (light therapy with a sunlamp) or medication	counseling or medication may be added to existing treatments for other illnesses

the signs
and
symptoms

the signs and symptoms

"THERE WAS A BATTLE IN MY HEAD."

Katherine's Story

Sometimes, Katherine, 14, felt wild and out of control. Other times, she was overwhelmed with sadness.

Everyone always thought I was weird. I remember being picked on all the way back in fourth grade. It really got to me. I'd hurry home and turn off all the lights in my room and bury myself under the bed covers for hours. Soon I stopped doing my homework. None of this seemed like a crisis to me. I was just lazy and irresponsible, right? And, hey, what little kid doesn't get bummed out by teasing?

Still, I began to see myself the way others did: I was weird.

By sixth grade, I'd drag myself to school in sweatpants every day. I didn't care about the way I looked or acted. In class, I'd feel this overwhelming urge to go wild. Part of me wanted to say mean things. Another part of me wanted to run and hide. There was a battle in my head. These two voices were shouting at each other. And there was the real me, in the middle, trying to stay in control.

But I wasn't in control. I was going downhill—fast.

Near the end of sixth grade, my mom called me into her room. I could tell she'd been crying. She put her arm around me and told me everything was going to be OK. She said I didn't have to lie anymore. She knew about all those missed homework assignments. She knew about my behavior in school. And she knew what was wrong with me. She had had the same problem. I was depressed.

Depressed? I didn't believe it. To me, depression was wearing black and writing moody poems. Depressed people were quiet. Sure, sometimes I felt sad about the way I acted. But I could be uncontrollably loud too. I fought with other kids and yelled at people. That's not depression.

*But guess what? Not all depression looks alike. My mom took me to a **psychologist**. She opened my eyes. She told me that people can be depressed in different ways. Some are sad and sulky. Some are angry. I had a kind of depression called bipolar disorder. BP makes you have wild mood swings. The highs are manic. And the lows are very dark.*

It's so hard to predict mood swings when you have bipolar disorder. Today, I see a psychologist and I take medications to keep my mood stable. But my BP isn't gone. It just looks different. When I'm feeling good, I have an inner peace. I dress in my own style—kinda preppy punk. But when my BP hits, I dye my hair blonde and wear makeup. I watch MTV all the time and expect the captain of the football team to invite me to prom. That's not the real Katherine. You might think you know what depression looks like. But don't make any assumptions. Depression will fool you.

"But I wasn't in control. I was going downhill—fast."

"Everyone thinks I'm the happiest person."

What Does Depression Look Like?

Some people are sad.
Some are angry.
Some can't sleep.
Others can't eat.
Could they all have depression?

The Many Faces of Depression

Samantha, 15, is bubbly and outgoing—everyone's best friend, she's the first person to talk to the new kid in school and the first to help with a homework problem. But she's the last person anyone suspected of being depressed.

"Everyone thinks I'm the happiest person," Samantha says. "You're not going to find me crying in the bathroom." But at home, Samantha lets her guard down. Deep periods of gloom settle over her, sometimes for seemingly no reason at all. They can last 20 minutes, a couple of hours, or even a few days. "If the kids at school saw me at home, sitting in the dark, crying my eyes out," she says, "they'd wonder if I was the same person."

Kevin, 15, first noticed his depression when he was four. In kindergarten, he couldn't sit still. "I'd tap my arm or my leg. I couldn't concentrate," he says. As he grew older, he developed new symptoms. He had trouble sleeping. Some days, he had so little energy he could barely make it to school.

"I never got really excited about anything," Kevin says.

Katherine, Samantha, and Kevin all had different symptoms. But each was suffering from depression. Depression has many signs (outward signals) and symptoms (internal feelings). Often the signs and symptoms of depression are the same: looking and feeling sad and hopeless; sleeping much less or much more than usual; crying for reasons that cannot be explained; or never wanting to do things that used to be fun.

The signs and symptoms of depression can affect every aspect of life: feelings, thoughts, behavior, and your physical health. For adolescents, these warning signs can show up as sulking, negativity, feeling misunderstood, and getting into trouble at school. But everyone who suffers from depression is different. Not all of their symptoms are alike. And you can't spot depressed people just by looking at them. So how do you know if you— or someone you know—is depressed?

TWELVE SIGNS
of Depression

People with depression usually have *two or more* of the following signs and symptoms lasting for two or more weeks:

1. Problems with sleep
2. Lack of energy
3. Problems with appetite and body weight
4. Headaches and stomachaches that do not go away
5. Problems with anger
6. Slowed motion, restlessness, or jittery patterns of movement
7. Feeling sad and empty
8. Feeling discouraged and hopeless
9. Feeling worthless and guilty
10. Lacking focus; being indecisive
11. Forgetting events that used to be considered important and special
12. Thinking or talking about how life has no meaning and is without hope

changes
in the body

Depression is a mental illness. But it can have very real physical symptoms. Here are a few physical symptoms of depression:

1 **Trouble falling asleep or staying asleep.** People with depression may wake up in the middle of the night every night and not be able to fall back asleep. Others may sleep too much. "I would stay awake all night with my mind racing 100 miles an hour," Katherine says of her episodes with depression.

2 **Fatigue and lack of energy.** People with depression may feel as if their arms and legs are too heavy to move. They may not be able to get out of bed in the morning, even if they are able to get the right amount of sleep at night. "I felt like there was a huge weight on me, holding me down to the mattress," says Shannon. "I literally could not move."

3 Too little or too much appetite.

People with depression may gain weight or lose weight even if their appetite does not become disturbed. When her depression was bad, Katherine binged on potato chips. But Shannon couldn't eat at all. At the height of her depression, she lost ten pounds in just two weeks.

4 Headaches and stomachaches that never go away.

Even if people with depression cannot describe these physical changes, the people around them may notice that these problems are affecting their everyday behavior.

changes
IN BEHAVIOR

People with depression may also experience changes in their interests, activities, and movements. Changes may include:

- Becoming bored and losing interest in people and things they used to care about and enjoy. They may not care about hobbies, games, sports, music, dating or spending time with friends.

- Stopping everyday activities and staying at home alone in bed, never wanting to take a shower, put on clean clothing, or go out for once enjoyable events. Kids may stop wanting to leave their home or go to school. Shannon stayed indoors for a week, unable to go to school or even get dressed. "Having my mom drive me to Wendy's was about as much as I could handle," she says. Katherine wore the same pair of sweatpants to school for weeks. Adults may stop wearing appropriate clothing, shopping for groceries, or going to work.

- Drinking alcohol, using street drugs, smoking cigarettes, or staying out all night. They may take reckless risks with bikes, skateboards, and cars.

- Moving more slowly, slumping over at times when they used to stand tall, straight, and strong. They may appear fidgety or jittery or restless at times when they used to seem focused and calm. Even as a kindergartener, Kevin was unable to sit still. He often tapped his foot or knocked his arm against the desk. What looked like childhood restlessness was really a sign of depression.

Have you spotted these signs in your friends? Your family? Yourself? Tell someone about it. Talk to your friends and family about your concerns. If you see signs of depression in yourself, tell your parents or mention it to a doctor, a teacher, or an adult you trust.

Changes in Feelings

Depression is linked to serious changes in emotions and feelings. People with depression experience not just everyday blues, but the grays and blacks of darker moods. These symptoms of depression often block people from going to the doctor for treatment.

feelings associated

• Sadness and emptiness

People with depression do not always feel the happiness and joy from everyday pleasures like eating, playing, laughing, and spending time with family and friends. They may seem to be tearful or crying all the time for reasons they cannot explain. "My family and friends would ask why I was crying," says Samantha. "I would tell them, 'I don't know!'"

• Anger

People with depression may be angry at others for reasons they cannot identify, understand, or explain. Often, people don't realize that irritability is a sign of depression. Even Samantha was surprised by her feelings. "Little things would get me very angry," she says. "Either I'd cry in my room about it or just start yelling at everyone. I knew people were just trying to help me or comfort me. But I couldn't stop myself."

They can feel so hopeless that they can't imagine anyone helping them. They can feel so tired and uncertain that they can't find the strength to ask for help. Changes in how people talk about themselves during depression are closely linked to how they feel about themselves.

WITH DEPRESSION

• Discouragement and hopelessness

People with depression cannot seem to remember that they used to have happy feelings and pleasures before their depression began. They worry that their feelings will continue to get worse, and they lose hope that anyone can help them feel better.

• Worthlessness and guilt

People with depression sometimes believe that they deserve their negative feelings. They seem to believe that they failed to work hard enough to achieve impossible goals, that they always make more mistakes than everyone else, and that everyone sees them as failures. Samantha had terrible thoughts about herself. "I always felt worthless and ugly," she says. "I'd look in the mirror and just hate myself."

Changes in Thoughts

Family and friends who notice the changes in behavior that indicate possible depression also may notice that these people think and talk about themselves in darker ways than they used to. Changes may include:

What's going on? I just can't focus.

thoughts that seem jumbled

People with depression may not be able to concentrate. They may not be able to make decisions. They may not be able to pass tests in subjects that used to be easy for them. They may not remember important things like birthday parties or their favorite television programs. Kevin was so fidgety that he could barely focus on his schoolwork.

I'm ugly. I'm stupid. I'm a loser. I'm a failure.

thoughts that are very negative

People with depression may say that they do not deserve to be healthy and happy. They may talk about running away from home. They may believe that medical treatment for depression will not work, or that it may work for others but not for them. They even may believe that no one wants them to get treatment or to feel better.

I'm nothing. I don't contribute anything to my family—or to my friends.

thoughts about death

Without treatment, the negative thoughts of depression may turn into thoughts about death and suicide. "Too many times those thoughts crossed my mind," Katherine says. "It's a very, very dark place to be." Talk of suicide is no joke.

Family and friends who hear people with depression expressing jumbled or negative thoughts need to encourage them to get treatment. People with depression who talk about death or suicide need to be taken very seriously. If a friend says something that worries you, tell a teacher or a parent. You aren't betraying a trust. You may be saving your friend's life. For more information, see pages 88–91.

time out for science

time out for science

"I NEVER REALLY THOUGHT OF DEPRESSION AS A DISEASE"

Kevin's Story

"It's all my dad's fault." Kevin, 15, is joking. Sort of. For ten years, Kevin has battled depression. It started in kindergarten when teachers noticed that Kevin couldn't sit still. He fidgeted in his chair. It grew worse as the years went on.

By the time the fifth grade rolled around, Kevin suffered from insomnia. He could barely pay attention in class. And friends started noticing his increasingly dark moods. Kevin never seemed to be happy or sad. Just ... blank.

"I never get very high over anything," he says. "I just keep at the same flat level. People would tell me to cheer up or try to smile. After awhile you start thinking there must be something wrong with you."

At home, Kevin's father knew all too well what was happening to his son. The symptoms were familiar. Kevin's father battled depression for years.

The Genetics of Depression

Have you heard the expression "It's all in the family"? That's not just true for intelligence, good looks, or even throwing a football. It can also be true for depression. Experts believe that depression can be passed along from parents. "If you have one parent with depression, you have about a 25 percent chance of having it, too," says Dr. Fassler. "If you have two parents with depression, your risk increases to about 75 percent."

Samantha's father was often hospitalized for depression. But she was still surprised when she recognized dark periods in herself. "I knew he suffered from it, but I never really thought of depression as a disease," Samantha says. "And I never thought of it as something I might have."

Katherine's mom never revealed that she had struggled with depression until Katherine was

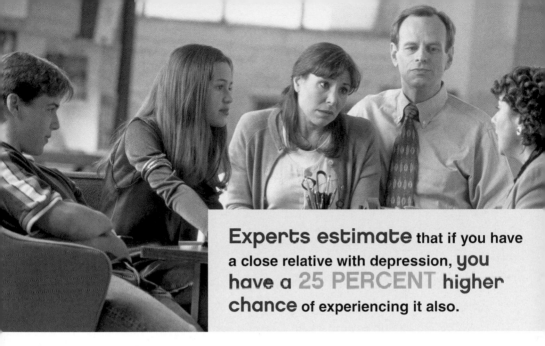

Experts estimate that if you have a close relative with depression, **you have a 25 PERCENT higher chance** of experiencing it also.

diagnosed with the same illness. "Looking back, it explains a lot," Katherine says. "It's sort of a relief to know that other people have dealt with this—and they are OK now."

Not everyone who has a genetic makeup for depression actually gets depressed. And there are a lot of people who have no family history who develop the condition anyway. "We inherit our ability to cope with stress," Fassler says. "If you have the right combination of genes, you are more likely to get depressed when placed under a lot of stress." Scientists realize that, while heredity is a factor in your mental health, it's not the only cause of depression.

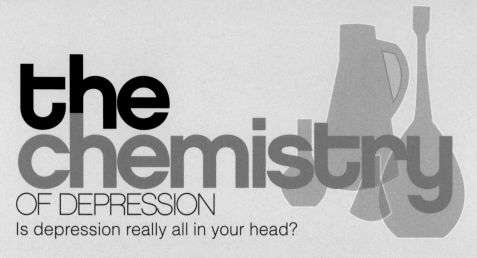

the chemistry
OF DEPRESSION

Is depression really all in your head?

You don't need an A in chemistry to understand depression. But if you really want to learn about the disease, a little science can't hurt. Don't worry. We'll make it as painless as possible. But to find out what's going on in our heads, we need to look into our brains, our genes, and all over our bodies.

If you've read anything about depression, you've probably come across the phrase *chemical imbalance*. Many people blame it for causing depression. But they probably don't know that a chemical imbalance is only a partial explanation for what causes depression. And what exactly is a chemical imbalance anyway?

It's common for people to say that the wrong mix of chemicals in your brain causes depression. And that's true—sort of. The way your brain works can be a factor in whether or not you develop depression. It's not the only reason—but it's one of the big ones.

There's a lot going on in your head. Or in your brain, actually. Your brain is constantly making chemicals that control the way you feel, act, and see the world around you.

Some of the most important chemicals are neurotransmitters and **hormones**. They transfer information and instructions from the brain to the body about energy, growth, sleep, digestion, hunger, happiness, and self-esteem.

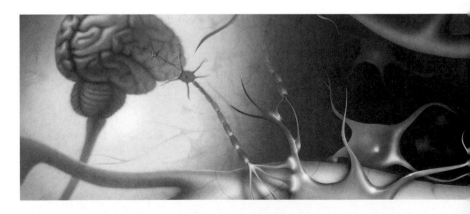

When Neurotransmitters Work Correctly

Neurotransmitters travel from neuron (nerve cell) to neuron throughout the body's nervous system. They move from the transmitting end of one neuron to the receiving end of the next neuron by swimming across an intercellular space called a synapse. Each neurotransmitter has its own unique molecular structure, carries its own unique neurochemical messages, and it docks with its own unique **neuroreceptor** as it travels along its neural pathway. When neurotransmitters work correctly, their neurochemical messages translate into moods and feelings clearly and right on time: "I feel happy"; "I feel safe"; "I feel sleepy"; "I feel excited"; or "I feel scared."

moods:

happy   scared   sleepy

When Neurotransmitters Get Out of Balance

Things can go wrong with the complex chain of events along neurotransmitter pathways. Neurotransmitters or neuroreceptors can act too quickly or too slowly. There can be a traffic jam in the synapses if there's too much of one neurotransmitter and not enough of another. That's when an imbalance may result, which can scramble our messages about moods and feelings.

Neurotransmitter imbalances can happen for many different reasons. Sometimes, genetics cause depression, but often depression results from environmental stresses such as life changes, peer pressure, violence, abuse, neglect, or trauma. These stressors can contribute to neurotransmitter imbalances and result in too little or too much energy, sleep, hunger, happiness, or even self-esteem. In other words, the imbalances can create the major symptoms of depression.

The most effective treatments for depression are those that address how neurotransmitter balances and imbalances affect people's feelings and behaviors. Sometimes, treatment may include prescription medication intended to help the body get its neurotransmitter system back to a healthier balance—and keep it that way.

Bipolar Disorder

Have you ever had a day where you feel like you are riding an emotional roller coaster? First, you're ecstatic over getting an A on the book report you worked so hard on. Then you plummet to the depths because your date for this weekend just canceled for no reason.

Welcome to Katherine's world. One minute, Katherine is the life of the party. She'll spend hours on her makeup and dance until her feet hurt. "I can just explode with energy," she says. "I can be like a supernova." But Katherine can burn out just as fast. "I'm not a party girl inside," she says. "Suddenly, I feel so bad about being in that crowd and disgusted with myself. I'll hate myself."

For Katherine, a roller-coaster ride isn't just normal teen life. Her mood fluctuations are signs of a serious illness called bipolar disorder. Originally called manic-depressive disorder, bipolar disorder creates a wild ride of moods that go from high (mania) to low (depression) and back again over a period of weeks, months, or years.

the highs
AND LOWS
of bipolar disorder

During a depressive low, people with bipolar disorder feel sad, hopeless, and lacking energy. They may stay in bed for days at a time and lose interest in school, sports, and friends. During a manic high, those feelings swing wildly. Suddenly they feel beyond happy. They're ecstatic. They are too confident. They feel like they can do anything and are ready to start a million new projects all at once. They are impatient, reckless, energetic, and wakeful. They might go days without sleep.

People with bipolar disorder often do not want to see a doctor for treatment during their manic highs. They feel far too superpowerful and superconfident and they prefer the highs to the hopelessness and sadness of their lows. But the superhighs of mania can cause serious harm to people with bipolar disorder and to their families and friends. Finding the right treatment is essential.

DEPRESSION
Can Be a
CHRONIC DISEASE

In a study of 851 people, interviewed first at age 19 and again at age 24, researchers discovered that 62.3 percent of those who reported having had depression before the age of 18 also experienced depression again during the ages of 19 to 24. Source: "Major Depression in Adolescence Can Reoccur in Adulthood and Diminish Quality of Life," American Psychological Association press release, August 24, 2003.

Experts say it's crucial for people to know the signs and symptoms of depression. People who have had depression should work with their therapist to recognize their triggers. Perhaps you become depressed when your life situation changes, such as your older brother leaving for college. Perhaps it's when you've suffered a loss, such as cutting ties with a friend. For others, it may be added stress, like a final exam on the same day as the state basketball championship game. If you know what sparks your depression, you might be able to stave off a crisis before it hits.

depression

Q&A

Depression is complex and confusing. Even scientists are stumped by some of the signs, symptoms, and treatments for the disease. So it's natural to have questions of your own. We asked the experts to help.

Q How do I know if I'm depressed—or if I'm just sad?

A It's not always easy to tell. "Depression is a very tough illness to diagnose," says Dr. Fassler. Sometimes depression looks like a bad day. You're blue. You have low levels of energy. Or you're just plain cranky. Kids with depression can have trouble sleeping, eating, or concentrating. The difference between depression and sadness, he says, is how long these feelings last—and how intense they become. "If you have new moods or behaviors that aren't going away for a couple of weeks and they are interfering with your schoolwork, the things you do with your friends, or your relationships, it could be depression," he says.

Q People say it's normal for teenagers to be moody. Is that true? Or am I depressed?

A It's true that teen brains are wired differently from adult brains. Your hormones and brain chemistry will assure that "teens naturally have more emotional turbulence," says William Beardslee, MD, Harvard Medical School. It can be hard to tell when you're experiencing growing pains—or if you are on the road to developing depression. Roughly one out of ten teens suffers significant depression before the age of 18. Girls, once they reach puberty, are twice as likely as boys to become depressed. Again, experts look for whether the symptoms interfere with your life and whether they last for an abnormally long time. "It's fine to be sad when your boyfriend or girlfriend breaks up with you," Beardslee says. "But if you can't go to school because of it, or if it's several months later and you are still crying every night, you should talk to someone."

Q I heard you have to take drugs if you're depressed. Can I get addicted to them?

A Each person's depression is different. And their treatment is different, too. "Everyone needs an individual plan," Beardslee says. "What works for one person may not work for another." Still, most people with ongoing depression will likely be prescribed some medication, possibly a type of drugs called antidepressants.

These drugs come with risks. Some studies suggest they can increase suicidal thoughts in a small number of young people. But most experts think that, when carefully monitored, they do more good than harm. "I believe young people should start with talking therapies [see page 61]. If those aren't sufficient, they should consider medications," Beardslee says. A doctor should help you understand the risks and benefits of these drugs. "We carefully monitor any young person on medication," Beardslee notes. Antidepressants aren't addictive. But in order for the drugs to be most effective, they must be taken over a period of time and at the correct dosage.

Q If I'm depressed now, will I always be depressed?

A No! People who get help usually feel better! (See Chapter 4.) However, you may be at a greater risk of developing depression again. That's why experts say it's important to find a good therapist who can help you recognize the signs and symptoms of the disease. "It helps to learn as much as you can about your own triggers and warning signs," Fassler says. With medications, doctors usually continue your prescription for three to six months after your symptoms go away. If they return, there's a good chance that you will need to take medication for a significant period of time.

"People who get help usually feel better!"

Q Do I have to go to a therapist if I'm depressed? It feels weird to talk about it.

A Most experts say talking with a counselor is a good idea. There are many different kinds of therapy and sometimes you need to try several before you find the one that's right for you. Cognitive-behavioral therapy, for example, helps you learn new ways to think about yourself, your behavior, and your illness. Not all therapy involves sitting in a doctor's office or lying on a couch. "With some kids, I read comic books all day," Fassler says. "With others, I shoot baskets. It's all about finding what's comfortable for you."

getting
help

getting help

"I DON'T WANT TO TALK TO ANYONE!"

Shannon Finds Help

Shannon didn't want to talk about her depression—until she found a therapist who helped her open up.

The thought of talking to someone about my problems turned me off. I didn't want to be a complainer. It's not like my parents are divorced or my little brother got hit by a bus. I'm just a kid who couldn't handle her schoolwork and breaking up with her boyfriend. I guess I thought a therapist might laugh at me. Or tell me to get over myself. She sees people with real illnesses and people who've had terrible tragedies in their family. I was just a whiny little kid.

At first, I went to a social worker. She diagnosed my depression almost immediately. Just knowing that I had an illness—that the way I was acting wasn't me—gave me a sense of freedom. Now I had a concrete problem to tackle. But I didn't click with the social worker. It wasn't her fault. She was nice, but I wasn't comfortable. She always asked me how I felt. I didn't know how to answer. I wasn't sure how I felt. I couldn't find the right words.

Eventually, my school counselor recommended a therapist. I was reluctant to go. If one therapist didn't work, why would another? I remember slumping in her chair, not expecting to feel better. The therapist said, "So you just broke up with your boyfriend and you haven't left the house in a week. You must feel like crap." I almost jumped out of my shoes. "Yes!" I said. Finally, someone understood me.

I see my therapist every week. And I actually look forward to it. She's really down to earth and approachable. We can talk about anything. I put a lot of pressure on myself. She helps ease the pressure. She's always on my side. Talking about my problems isn't the whole answer. I also take medication. And I still struggle with episodes of depression. But when I walk into her office each week, I know it's a place where I can relax. It's a place where no one judges me. And I can just be me.

How Many Teenagers
RECEIVE TREATMENT
for Depression?

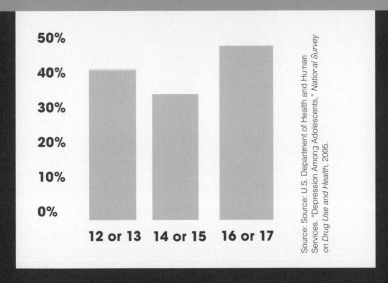

Source: Source: U.S. Department of Health and Human Services. "Depression Among Adolescents." *National Survey on Drug Use and Health,* 2005.

Depression is treatable. Many teens who find the right treatment feel better. But fewer than half of the teenagers who reported having depression in 2004 were treated for it. If depression is left untreated, it may become life threatening or deepen into a **chronic**, lifelong condition.

gettingwell

Depression doesn't always go away on its own. It's important to find the right doctors and the right treatment to help yourself feel better as quickly as possible.

Start with the Right Doctors

Many people with depression receive treatment from their primary care physicians, but physicians often refer patients to psychiatrists or psychologists. These professionals have special training in the diagnosis and treatment of depression and other mental health disorders.

There are different kinds of mental health experts. Not all provide the same services. Patients and their families should seek the advice of their physician when deciding which one of these is right for them:

- **Therapists and counselors** are usually social workers or licensed mental health professionals who specialize in **psychotherapy**, which is sometimes known as talk therapy because it involves patients talking about their problems. Therapists may be social workers, nurse practitioners, counselors, psychologists, or psychiatrists.
- **Psychologists** are mental health professionals with doctoral degrees. They conduct research, testing, and psychotherapy.
- **Psychiatrists** are medical doctors who specialize in treating mental, emotional, or behavioral disorders. Psychiatrists can prescribe drugs and other medical treatments in addition to conducting psychotherapy.

Get the Right Diagnosis

Diagnosing the specific form of depression affecting each patient is the essential first step any doctor takes before prescribing any treatments. Reaching a diagnosis may require multiple visits and may include:

- **Physical examination:** What part(s) of the brain and the body is/are involved? Are other medical conditions causing or contributing to the depression? Is medication necessary?

- **Patient's medical history:** Does the patient have any allergies? Immunizations? Prior illnesses? Prior episodes of depression? Thoughts of death or suicide?

- **Family medical history:** What signs of depression have been observed in the patient? Which illnesses affected parents, grandparents, brothers, and sisters? Did any of them have depression or bipolar disorder?

- **Screening inventory:** What words can patients use on a written questionnaire to describe accurately their complex feelings, thoughts, and behaviors?

choose
THE RIGHT
treatments

Extensive research demonstrates that the most effective treatment for depression is a COMBINATION of prescription medication and psychotherapy. The medication helps make the symptoms of depression less severe so that the patient can talk to and work with a psychotherapist. Working with a psychotherapist can help the patient understand the depression and learn effective ways to cope with it.

THINGS YOU CAN DO
If You Have Depression

 Talk to a parent or older family member. He or she might be able to help you find help.

 Go to your school counselor or psychologist and get a referral to a mental health specialist for extra counseling and support services.

 Go to your doctor. Tell the doctor that you have symptoms of depression and that you know it is a real illness that needs medical treatment.

 Take a chance on hope. You may feel now that life is hopeless. But keep telling yourself that that's your depression talking. You can and will feel better.

What Is Therapy?

Psychotherapy is also known as talk therapy.
Psychotherapy is when a person talks to a mental
health professional—a psychiatrist, psychologist,
social worker, or counselor—about the way he or
she feels and thinks. Experts have long hailed the
benefits of therapy. It can help change negative
thoughts and behavior patterns. A good therapist
can also help you be more aware of problems
in your life—which you might have ignored,
forgotten, or blocked out—that are impacting your
daily functioning.

Most of the young people in this book have
experienced some form of therapy. And most say
it helped them overcome their depression. "I love
therapy," Katherine says. "It feels so good to talk
to someone who understands me." In fact, her
therapist has helped her recognize the situations
that trigger her depression. "Now I know what to
look for, so I can cut it off before anything serious
happens," Katherine says.

"It feels so good to talk to someone who understands me."

Psychotherapy Realities

OK, so the idea of sitting in an office talking about your feelings turns you off. It can take some time to get used to therapy. "At first, I always felt like I was whining," says Shannon. "Yeah, my boyfriend broke up with me and I failed a big math test. Blah blah blah. I thought I was complaining."

Psychotherapy takes place most often in the office of a psychologist, social worker, or mental health counselor. Therapy sessions may be private, with just the therapist and the patient, or they may involve the patient's family or a support group of several patients suffering from depression. Many people work out a therapy schedule that mixes individual sessions with therapy groups.

But all therapists are different. And they find different ways to connect with their patients. Dr. Fassler talks to some kids in his office. With some, he draws pictures. With others, he shoots baskets. "It's up to the patient to come to me," he says. "But once he's there, it's up to me to find a way to make him comfortable—and to keep him coming back."

Psychotherapy USUALLY includes:

- quiet, safe, and comforting discussions between patient and therapist
- curtains and soundproofing to protect your privacy
- comfortable chairs, couches, and carpeted floors to sit or lounge on
- paints, sand trays, or stuffed animals
- photographs, journals, or diaries
- real animals trained as therapy dogs

Psychotherapy NEVER includes:

- needles or injections
- anything that causes physical pain
- alcohol or anything that numbs you
- negative or condemning comments
- blame or guilt

CHOOSING
the Right Psychotherapist

Parents, doctors, school counselors, and the Web sites in the Resources section can help teens with depression find a good therapist to work with. But only the person with depression can decide if that therapist is the right one. Consider these factors:

Knowledge: Do you believe that this therapist remembers and understands what it's like to be a teen, with or without depression?

Honesty: Do you believe that this therapist will tell you the truth about your illness and your treatment?

Respect: Do you believe that this therapist will treat you respectfully, even when you need to say things that adults don't like to hear?

Ask the therapist about each of these factors during your first few visits and listen very carefully to the answers. If the responses give you hope that you can trust this person to help make you feel better, then you have found the right therapist.

Support: Do you believe that this therapist will support the decisions you want to make about your illness and your treatment?

Kindness and empathy: Do you believe that this therapist understands what you're going through and cares about helping you to feel better?

Training and experience: Does the therapist have solid training? Does he or she have experience with other patients?

How Cognitive-Behavioral Therapy Works

Cognitive-behavioral therapy (CBT) is one of the most effective forms of psychotherapy for depression because it focuses both on thoughts (cognition) and on behavior. CBT can help people learn new ways to think about themselves, their behavior, and their illness. For example:

- People whose depression makes them think that they are only worthless failures can learn techniques to remind themselves of all the times they did things right.
- People whose depression makes them think that they must achieve impossible goals can learn techniques for changing impossible goals into realistic ones.
- People whose depression makes them think that no one cares for them can learn to recognize the signs of caring and support that may be all around them but are clouded from view by the depression.

Many research studies have shown that the long-term effectiveness of CBT is far greater than treatment with medication alone.

CHANGING Thoughts, Feelings, and Behaviors Through CBT

Before Treatment

Prior to treatment, a thought pattern may be creating a chain of events that contributes to depression:

EXPERIENCE	THOUGHT	FEELINGS	BEHAVIORS
Report card is sent home.	"If I don't get all As, I'm a complete failure."	Sad, hopeless, worthless	Isolating from friends, crying, yelling at siblings

As a Result of Treatment

Through cognitive-behavioral therapy, new thought patterns can be learned and used to create a whole new chain of events, with little evidence of depression:

EXPERIENCE	THOUGHT	FEELINGS	BEHAVIORS
Report card is sent home.	"I did the best I could, and my grades don't define me as a person."	Confident, happy, hopeful	Making plans to go out, having fun, helping sibling with homework

The Vocabulary of
PSYCHOTHERAPY

Therapeutic alliance:
the safe and trusting relationship that therapist and patient must create so they can discuss negative thoughts, feelings, and behaviors openly with each other

Therapeutic goals or contract: a clearly stated
agreement between therapist and patient about what the patient wants to achieve. The patient may say the goal is "not to be depressed," but the therapist may suggest a more specific goal, such as eliminating symptoms, finding self-confidence, or learning optimism.

Homework: opportunities to practice new behaviors between appointments with the therapist. For a patient who has lost interest in favorite activities, a homework assignment might be to watch two movies or play two video games. Sometimes the therapist will give the patient tokens or rewards for accomplishing the therapy goals.

Mental tune-ups: a return to therapy. Patients often feel ready to end psychotherapy treatment when symptoms improve. But if the symptoms return because life throws a curveball— or just because symptoms sometimes return—the therapist will welcome the patient back. A return to therapy doesn't mean the initial treatment was unsuccessful. Most often, it just means that it's time for a "tune-up." Mental tune-ups are one of the best parts of the therapeutic alliance.

finding the right treatment

Finding the right treatment

"WHEN MY TREATMENT IS GOING WELL, I KNOW THAT THINGS ARE GOING TO BE OKAY."

Katherine Finds Help

Katherine has had success combining therapy with medication.

The first time I walked into a therapist's office, I immediately knew I was going to like it. Before I could say a word, I broke out into sobs. I had been holding it in for so long, it felt good to let it out. I still see a psychologist to help me handle my depression and bipolar disorder. But I've also found that talking about my problem isn't enough. A big part of my depression is fixing the wiring in my brain. And I can't do that on my own.

I was first diagnosed with depression in the summer of sixth grade. My psychologist immediately prescribed medication. I'm on mood stabilizers to deal with the highs and lows of being bipolar. And I take antidepressants, too. Yeah, it sounds like a lot of pills, but believe me, I'm a lot better with the meds than I am without them.

The medicine doesn't make me feel weird. It makes me feel more like me. When my treatment is going well—both my therapy and my medication—I know that things are going to be OK. Don't get me wrong. It's not as easy as popping a pill and feeling better. In fact, it took about a year and a half to figure out which meds worked for me.

Dealing with depression can be a long road. I might be dealing with this for my whole life. I might always be on meds. And that's OK. It's part of who I am. I don't see myself as a sick person. I see myself as one of the strongest people I know.

"Dealing with depression can be a long road."

what are PSYCHIATRIC medications?

If I'm depressed, will I have to take medications? Can these drugs harm me? How do I know when they work? Psychiatric medication can be confusing. But don't worry. We will answer your medication questions.

Because depression is linked to imbalances in the body's complex chemistry of genes, proteins, hormones, and neurotransmitters, sometimes medication is the fastest and most effective treatment for it.

Antidepressants target the body's neurologic system, focusing on the neurotransmitters serotonin, norepinephrine, and dopamine, which are substances that transfer biochemical instructions and messages from the transmitting end of one neuron to the receiving end of the next. When serotonin and other neurotransmitters work correctly, we send ourselves enough "I'm happy," "I'm safe," and "I can handle this" messages. When neurotransmitters get out of balance so do our feelings, moods, and ability to cope. That's when we may need medication to get us back into balance.

How Does Antidepressant Medication Work?

Medications like fluoxetine and sertraline are **selective serotonin reuptake inhibitors** (**SSRIs**) that target the neurotransmitter serotonin, keeping it active in the synaptic gap between neurons—maintaining feelings of happiness, comfort, and safety in the proper balance to counteract feelings of depression.

Side Effects of Medication

Sometimes psychiatric medications cause unwanted side effects, especially if they interact badly with food, alcohol, or another prescription medication. Unwanted side effects may include nausea, dizziness, high blood pressure, liver problems, muscle problems, or even thoughts of suicide.

It is essential for people taking medication to be monitored by their doctors on a regular basis. The doctor can check for side effects, adjust medication if necessary, or even alert the patient to newly discovered medications with fewer side effects.

Finding the Right Medication

Medication to treat depression usually is prescribed by a psychiatrist. It may take several tries before the psychiatrist finds the most effective medication for any individual case of depression. It may take two to four weeks before the medication starts to take effect noticeably.

Once the right medication or combination of medications starts working, the patient may need to continue on the medication for about a year, or possibly longer if the patient has been diagnosed with chronic (long-term) depression or bipolar disorder. It is essential that patients follow the doctor's instructions about taking medication and always discuss with the doctor when and how to stop taking it.

Not all therapies work for all people. Some people benefit from psychotherapy. Others from medication. And still others from both. Talk with your doctor to work out a plan that works best for you. "Everyone needs a treatment plan that's individualized to a child and a family," says Dr. Fassler.

does
TREATMENT
work?

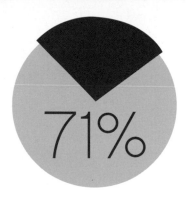

A 2004 study reported that 71 percent of individuals treated for depression with a combination of medication (an antidepressant called Prozac or fluoxetine) and cognitive-behavioral therapy experienced a reduction in symptoms.

Source: Richard M. Glass, MD, "Treatment of Adolescents with Major Depression," *Journal of the American Medical Association* 292 (2004): 807–820.

Eighty percent of people who seek treatment for depression are treated successfully.

Source: Suicide Awareness Voices of Education (*www.save.org*).

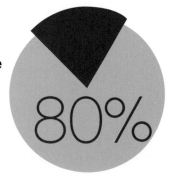

Rx Depression

Prescription medications have complex chemical names and generic names, but they also have brand names that are trademarked by the pharmaceutical companies that sponsor research and development. Some of the better-known medications used today to treat depression and bipolar disorder are:

GENERIC NAME	BRAND NAME
bupropion	Wellbutrin
citalopram	Celexa
divalproex	Depakote
duloxetine	Cymbalta
escitalopram	Lexapro
fluoxetine	Prozac/Sarafem
gabapentin	Neurontin
paroxetine	Paxil/Pexeva
sertraline	Zoloft
venlafaxine	Effexor

DOES
Saint-John's-Wort
WORK?

Many people believe that an herbal remedy called
Saint-John's-wort (*Hypericum perforatum*) is also
an effective treatment for depression because it is
believed to target the same neurotransmitters as
prescription medications. Researchers do not yet
have conclusive proof of its effectiveness, and some
studies have found that Saint-John's-wort has
NO IMPACT ON DEPRESSIVE SYMPTOMS. Researchers
do know that it may cause side effects in adults
taking other medications, so they recommend talking
to a doctor before using it or any other over-the-
counter medication. Children, teens, and pregnant
women should avoid Saint-John's-wort entirely.

other ways to counteract
DEPRESSION

Exercise

Exercise is one of the easiest treatments for depression. It gets the heart pumping and the neurotransmitters moving. "Runner's high" is a common term for the happier mood that many people feel after vigorous aerobic exercise. Other ways that exercise may have a positive impact on depression include:

- enhanced body image;
- increased self-confidence from meeting a goal;
- social support from an exercise group or team activity;
- distraction from day-to-day worries.

Phototherapy

Special lights and lamps can help people with seasonal affective disorder (SAD) maintain even moods during the darkest months of winter when there isn't enough daylight.

Support Groups

Support groups and self-help groups also help people with depression. Members of the groups exchange information about the disorder and about current research on treatment and medication. Support group members help one another develop strategies for living with the symptoms of depression and for coping with the need for continuous therapy or medication. Support groups also can help family members adjust to living with a person experiencing depression.

Acupuncture

Acupuncture is a treatment in which highly trained professionals—called acupuncturists—insert special needles at specific locations in the skin. Using principles of Chinese medicine that link health and illness to energy flow throughout the body, acupuncturists use needles to rebalance energy flow that has become unbalanced. The effects of acupuncture may be similar to the runner's high of aerobic exercise and indirectly help with depression.

Mindfulness and Meditation

Mindfulness is an idea that dates back to ancient Asian philosophies. Achieving mindfulness through meditative practices helps one learn to focus on living in the present moment and learn to see thoughts and feelings as possibilities, not facts. Mindfulness often is used in conjunction with cognitive-behavioral therapy, because it helps people learn how to accept what cannot be changed. Paradoxically, practitioners of mindfulness sometimes discover that acceptance can make it easier to act in new and different ways.

Animal-Assisted Therapies

Four-legged therapists are growing in popularity as research continues to prove their effectiveness. Trained therapy dogs and other animals now participate in regularly scheduled visits to hospitals and nursing homes.

Stigma and Prejudice

Depression sufferers have heard these same tired lines again and again—even from friends, family, and teachers. Stigma and prejudice have long been associated with mental illness. And there's nothing worse than being told that a genuine illness is a sign of weakness or failure.

It's all in your head!

"Some people don't look at depression as an illness," says Shannon. "They think you are just being moody or lazy. They think it's a weakness and you should be able to pull yourself out of it."

Depression can be a hard disease to diagnose. But even when a young person tells someone that he might be depressed, not everyone is quick to take him or her seriously. Instead of offering to help, an adult may think a teen can just "snap out of it"—a wrong-headed idea that frustrates mental health professionals. "If a child had a headache for two weeks, his parents

Snap out of it!

wouldn't expect him to snap out of it. They'd send him to a doctor," Fassler says. "But there is still a feeling that depression isn't serious and it will go away by itself."

Many kids are afraid to tell someone how they feel. That keeps teens from admitting they have a depression problem—and seeking help for it.

Katherine is open about her depression. Sometimes she gets supportive reactions and sometimes she doesn't. Other kids find that they are far from alone. They discover that other teens, including some of their closest friends, also deal with depression. "My mom doesn't want me to tell anybody about my depression. She thinks they will treat me differently," Shannon says. "But when I started telling people I was in therapy, many of my friends would say, 'Yeah, I see someone, too.' They had been going for years and I never knew."

strategies
for Getting Past
barriers
to treatment

1 Learn the signs and symptoms of depression. Be on the lookout for changes in your mood that are intense and long lasting. If sad thoughts have been lingering for too long, it's probably time to stop pretending they'll go away on their own.

2 Talk about it. Tell a friend, parent, or teacher. It can be hard to open up, but telling someone how you feel can make you feel better. Katherine first told a friend about her depression in sixth grade. "I was really nervous," she says. "But she was great. She said it explained the way I was acting. She wanted to know if she could help. It was like a huge weight off my shoulders."

3 Don't worry if it doesn't come out just right. It can be hard to find the right words to describe sadness, hopelessness, or anger. Shannon could never explain how she felt to her friends and family. "I wasn't sure myself, so how could I tell them?" she says. Eventually, a therapist helped her express her feelings.

4 Talk to your parents about seeing a professional for help. If asking to see a psychiatrist or psychotherapist is too intimidating or too expensive, then ask to see a school counselor or a regular family doctor.

Numbing the Pain

For some teens, depression can lead to drugs and alcohol abuse.

When the pain of depression becomes overwhelming, too many teens attempt to drown it through drugs and alcohol. Experts like Dr. Beardslee call that behavior "self-medicating."

"Some kids with depression feel so bad that they try to feel nothing at all," Beardslee says. Drugs and alcohol can seem like a way to cope with depression. But they can lead to deeper problems. Alcohol is a depressant. While some people think it makes them happier, it actually increases their depression. Many drugs are highly addictive. "If you're using drugs or alcohol to relieve your pain, you are just trading one set of problems for another," Beardslee says.

"If you're using drugs or alcohol to relieve your pain, you are just trading one set of problems for another."

SELF-MEDICATING
for Depression

A 2004 study reported that teens who had depression were nearly twice as likely to use alcohol, cigarettes, and street drugs as teens who did not have depression.

100%

80%

60%

40%

20%

0%

■ **Abusers with depression**

□ **Abusers without depression**

Source: U.S. Department of Health and Human Services. "Depression among Adolescents," *National Survey on Drug Use and Health*, 2005.

Teen abusers of alcohol

Teen abusers of street drugs

Teen abusers of cigarettes

A Terrible Despair

Shannon fights a daily battle with her depression. Some days she feels strong, but other days she's stuck in a very dark place, overwhelmed with feelings of sadness and despair. Before she began treatment, Shannon had to deal with thoughts of suicide. Suicidal thoughts are always to be taken very seriously.

WARNING signs

Some of the warning signs that a friend or family member is having destructive thoughts are similar to the signs of depression:

- Chronic problems with sleep, appetite, energy, and sadness
- Loss of interest in friends, family, activities, and pleasures
- Feeling sad, empty, discouraged, hopeless, and worthless

But there are other signs that can indicate a person may be in serious danger:

- A significant drop in school performance
- A sudden crisis at school or home
- A serious change in behavior

- Irrational or bizarre behavior
- Running away from home
- Acting recklessly and violently
- Acquiring guns or weapons
- Making threats to commit suicide
- Dropping hints: "I wonder whether getting hit by a car would hurt me"
- Talking about dying: "You wouldn't even miss me if I weren't around"
- Preparing for dying—for example, making a will or giving away one's belongings
- Having a friend or family member die of suicide
- Having made a prior attempt at suicide

These warning signs are serious.

It is essential to get help as quickly as possible. Contact a responsible adult, a doctor, a counselor, a coach, or a suicide hotline for immediate assistance. Conversation about suicide, especially from someone who has tried suicide in the past, is a genuine 911 emergency.

Good Friends Get Help

People who are thinking about suicide often talk about it with their friends. They may ask them to keep it a secret. Friends may fear they are betraying a trust if they ask an adult for help. Helping a friend get treatment for suicidal feelings—even when that friend is so upset that he or she does not want treatment—is always the right thing to do.

WHAT TO DO
in a crisis

Here are steps you can take to help when there is talk of suicide:

1 Encourage your friend to tell a parent, doctor, school counselor, coach, or a suicide hotline.

2 If he or she is unwilling, take the initiative to contact the responsible adult or suicide hotline yourself.

3 If there is an immediate danger of suicide, call 911 for help.

Making Your Peace with Depression

Depression can be lifelong. But as the teens in this book prove, it doesn't have to control your life.

Depression is a treatable disease. With the right therapy and medication, it can be controlled. After getting help, some teens never have another episode of depression. Others learn how to manage their illness. The four teens you met in this book realize depression may always be a part of their lives. In their own words, they talk about how they learned that depression can have a happy ending.

Shannon, 18

Some of the differences are dramatic. I have the strength and energy to do my schoolwork. I don't get panic attacks when a project is due. I no longer have periods when I just can't leave the house. I've learned my triggers and my personal workload. I have a lot of interests. But I now know I shouldn't take all AP classes and be on the ski team and work on big art projects—all at the same time!

Other changes are more subtle. When I was feeling bad, I could never seem to get over things. I couldn't move on. It didn't matter if it was something small, like a friend making a nasty comment, or something big, like my boyfriend breaking up with me. I could intellectualize it and convince myself that it wasn't the end of the world. But it still felt like my life was collapsing around me. Everyone feels bad about breaking up with a boyfriend. But the difference between being sad and being depressed is that the bad feelings don't go away. They take over your life.

Now, on a good day, I can take things in stride. On a bad day, I can say, "Oh, well, I'll go home, I'll listen to my favorite mix for half an hour, and I'll feel better." It doesn't sound like much. But here's the best part: I actually do!

Katherine, 14

All summer, I was out of bed at 8 a.m. I had my running shoes on. I jogged for miles. By the time I got home, I was sweaty and out of breath. I've never felt so good in my life! I joined the cross-country team. I'm in training for the season. But running isn't just a sport. It's also like therapy. Those summer mornings, I felt peaceful and calm. My mind was at ease. I could think about my day. Or I could think about nothing at all.

A year ago, I was all over the place. I stayed up late every night. My mind raced at 100 miles an hour. I was really low on myself. I thought I was stupid and weird. I guess I hated myself.

There's so much that goes into controlling my depression. There's therapy and medication. There's eating right and getting a good night's sleep. Exercise helps 110 percent, too. I've learned my triggers. I know who I want to be. I want to be that kid you see jogging on the sidewalk early on a Saturday morning. I feel my muscles straining, my blood pumping. I feel peaceful. I feel, well, happy.

Kevin, 15

Most people have no idea how to deal with me. They act weird around me, like they can't find something to say. Even when I was a little kid, I never got excited when someone gave me a present. I'd be like, "Oh, cool. Thanks." It's not that I didn't like the gifts. That's just the way I react to everything.

I'm not unhappy. It's more of an energy thing. My meds help me focus and stay in control. I can concentrate on my schoolwork now. When I'm off the medicine, I talk more, and I get really twitchy. People notice. I don't think a lot about why I'm like this. You turn on the TV and you see people who are a lot worse off than I am. Stuff happens to everyone. That's just life. I'm like everybody else. I wish people would understand that.

Samantha, 15

My glass is half full now. Or maybe half empty. About half the time I feel like I can deal with my depression. I'm happier. I have a great support system. My family and friends are really cool. I like my therapist. I'm taking my medications twice a day. It's kind of a drag, but it helps me feel stable. Most days, I'm OK.

But everyone has bad days. And mine are worse than most. I can feel dark periods coming on—sometimes for no reason. They can last for as little as 20 minutes or as long as a few days.

From what people tell me, depression doesn't leave you. So I better get used to it. I like to think I'm in recovery. No matter how bad your depression gets, there's always hope. That's kind of what gets me through the day. I'm a big believer in hope.

SOURCES YOU CAN TRUST

- Your doctor, therapist, or mental health counselor
- Web sites with .gov, .org, and .edu domain names that are supervised by clinical psychologists, counselors, physicians, and researchers. For example:
  - *www.nimh.nih.gov*: National Institute of Mental Health
  - *www.nami.org*: National Alliance on Mental Illness
  - *www.apa.org*: American Psychological Association
  - *www.KidsHealth.org*: Nemours Foundation
- Books and magazines published under the supervision of psychologists and medical professionals
- Books and magazines recommended by a school counselor, a school library media specialist, or a public librarian
- Books and magazines with recent publication dates. Mental health information becomes obsolete at a faster pace than most other information. If the information is more than one or two years old, look for something more up-to-date.

SOURCES TO BE WARY OF

- Web sites with .com domain names. These dot-coms are sponsored by private corporations and pharmaceutical companies that want to sell you medications and special treatment programs. The information may be accurate, but its main purpose may be profit, not wellness. Approach dot-com information with caution.
- Friends or adults who try to pressure you into decisions that make you uncomfortable.

ADJUSTMENT
Strategies at Home

FOR THE PERSON WITH DEPRESSION:

- Continue with your treatment plan.
- Reach out to friends, grandparents, and community members who can support you and your family during treatment for depression.

FOR FRIENDS AND FAMILY:

- Remember that the person with depression still loves you even if he or she cannot show it.
- Remember that you are not to blame for depression. Depression is a medical condition that requires treatment.
- Understand that the person with depression may be ashamed of the illness and its symptoms. Unpleasant feelings are an important component of depression.
- Understand that the person with depression may be worrying about you, especially if he or she is a parent who is unable to spend as much time with you as before.
- Ask if you can go to a therapy session. Ask the therapist to answer your questions about depression.
- Ask for regular family meetings to discuss the depression, the treatment, and ways family members can help during times of severe illness.
- Stay focused on living your own life.

ADJUSTMENT
Strategies at School

During treatment, it often helps for parents, teachers, and the principal to create an individualized education plan (IEP) that can make it possible for students with depression to stay in school and still graduate on time with their friends. An IEP may include:

- a later start or an earlier end to the school day
- two sets of textbooks: one for home and one for school
- recorded books for concentration problems during reading
- reduced homework or extended deadlines when energy is low
- one-on-one work with a teacher's aide
- tutoring during hospitalizations and other school absences
- accommodations for high-stakes tests
- regular sessions with a school psychologist or social worker
- identifying a "safe place" where the student can go when feeling overwhelmed
- summer day camp or summer school to help keep up with the curriculum
- therapeutic day schools and residential treatment centers as a transition back to regular school
- assistance with transitions from high school to college or career

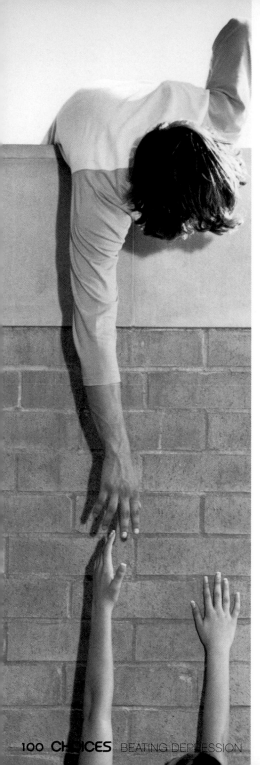

How to Help a Friend Who Has Depression

Kevin has heard it before. When his depression hits, friends and teachers try to talk him out of it. Just cheer up, they say. Put a smile on your face. Snap out of it. "I hate when people tell me that I should get over this and be happy," the 15-year-old says. "I want to say, 'Don't you think I've tried that?'"

Many young people know very little about depression. They may believe a friend with depression is trying to get attention. Or they think they can cheer up their friend by taking him to the movies. No matter how good your intentions, you can't snap a friend out of a depressive state.

steps
to take to help
a friend with depression

1 Try to be with your friend, even though it might not be easy. People with depression tend to feel as if they are all alone.

2 Don't think you can solve their problems by being overly cheery—or by vowing to cheer them up. Your friend may feel you aren't taking the problem seriously.

3 Don't blame them. They don't want to be depressed. And they can't just "snap out of it." Depression is no one's fault.

4 Don't get angry. It's nothing personal if your friend doesn't respond to your help.

5 Get adult help. If your friend talks about hurting himself, or you're worried for any other reason, talk to your parents, your friend's parents, or your school counselor. It's not a betrayal of trust to keep a friend safe.

Managing Your Feelings

If you have depression, then you already know that dark moods and feelings are part of the illness. If someone you love or care about is the one with depression, then you may be surprised by the negative reactions you are feeling about someone else's illness.

Anger, Disappointment, Frustration

Anger, disappointment, and frustration are all natural emotions, especially when a serious illness occurs. It's natural to want people with depression to feel better right away so that life can get back to "normal" for everyone involved. We don't want them to have dark thoughts, we don't want them to sleep all day every day, we don't want them drinking too much or using drugs, and we certainly don't want them to harm themselves.

Understanding and accepting our own negative emotions about depression requires the same kind of strength, patience, and support that people with depression need to stick to their treatment plans. Both take a long time and a lot of hard work.

LEARNING
optimism

"Learned optimism" and "learned helplessness" are terms linked to the work of psychologist Martin Seligman, who observed that people with depression often endure their illness passively, without even trying to get treatment. This is especially true for people whose depression may be a reaction to abuse or injury.

People with learned helplessness often behave as if they will never escape from depression's dark feelings. But if they were able to learn to react to their illness with helplessness and hopelessness, they can also learn optimism, which is the best medicine in the world. Optimism can help people understand that treatment for depression can lighten the heavy feelings of sadness, helplessness, hopelessness, and discouragement and can help any of us find our way back to lives filled with friendship, love, creativity, and joy.

antidepressants—prescription medications that may be used along with psychotherapy to treat depression

bipolar disorder—formerly called manic-depressive disorder, this causes cycles of major depression that alternate with extreme energy highs

chronic—lasting a long period of time

dopamine—a neurotransmitter that researchers have linked to depression

genetics—the study of DNA, chromosomes, genes, and inheritance patterns; many cases of depression are linked to genetic causes and tend to run in families, passing from parent to child in the same manner as skin color, eye color, and size

hormones—chemicals produced by the endocrine (glandular) system to carry messages to all the organs, transferring information and instructions from the brain about body processes like growth, sleep, and digestion

neuroreceptor—a location at the receiving end of a neuron that recognizes a specific neurotransmitter or medication and allows it to attach to the neuron

neurotransmitters—chemicals produced by the nervous system to carry messages from neuron to neuron, transferring information and instructions from the brain to the body about thoughts, emotions, and behaviors

norepinephrine—a neurotransmitter that researchers have linked to depression

psychiatrists—medical doctors who specializes in treating people who have mental disorders that affect the mind and the body

psychologist—a researcher who studies behaviors or a counselor who specializes in treating people whose mental disorders affect their behavior and social interactions

psychotherapist—a mental health counselor, social worker, psychologist, or doctor who helps individuals or groups of people in "talk therapy"

psychotherapy—often called "talk therapy," psychotherapy helps people understand their own thoughts, feelings, behaviors, and relationships with others; psychotherapy is one of the most effective treatments for depression and is often prescribed along with medication

selective serotonin reuptake inhibitors (SSRIs)—forms of antidepressant medications that are prescribed when the body cannot produce enough serotonin or cannot keep its serotonin active and available in the body; SSRIs help the body use its serotonin more effectively

serotonin—a neurotransmitter that researchers have linked to depression

Books for Teens

Allen, Jon. *Coping with Depression: From Catch-22 to Hope.* Washington DC: American Psychiatric Publishing, 2006.

Anderson, Neil T. *Stomping Out Depression.* New York: Regal Books, 2001.

Cobain, Bev. *When Nothing Matters Anymore: A Survival Guide for Depressed Teens.* Minneapolis: Free Spirit, 1998.

Desetta, Al, and Sybil Wolin, eds. *The Struggle to Be Strong: True Stories by Teens About Overcoming Tough Times.* Minneapolis: Free Spirit, 2000.

Books for Adults

Beardslee, William R. *Out of the Darkened Room: When a Parent Is Depressed: Protecting the Children and Strengthening the Family.* Boston: Little Brown, 2002.

Empfield, Maureen. *Understanding Teenage Depression: A Guide to Diagnosis, Treatment, and Management.* New York: H. Holt, 2001.

Fassler, David G., and Lynne S. Dumas. *Help Me, I'm Sad: Recognizing, Treating, and Preventing Childhood and Adolescent Depression.* New York: Penguin Books, 1997.

Griffith, Gail. *Will's Choice: A Suicidal Teen, a Desperate Mother, and a Chronicle of Recovery.* New York: HarperCollins, 2005.

Koplewicz, Harold S. *More Than Moody: Recognizing and Treating Adolescent Depression.* New York: Putnam, 2002.

Online Sites & Organizations

American Academy of Child and Adolescent Psychiatry
3615 Wisconsin Avenue NW
Washington, DC 20016
202/966-7300
www.aacap.org

American Psychiatric Association
1000 Wilson Boulevard
Suite 1825
Arlington, VA 22209
703/907-7300
www.psych.org
http://HealthyMinds.org

American Psychological Association
750 First Street NE
Washington, DC 20002
800/374-2721
www.apa.org

Depression and Bipolar Support Alliance
730 North Franklin Street
Suite 501
Chicago, IL 60610
800/826-3632
www.dbsalliance.org

Families for Depression Awareness
395 Totten Pond Road
Suite 404
Waltham, MA 02451
781/890-0220
www.familyaware.org

National Alliance on Mental Illness
2107 Wilson Boulevard
Suite 300
Arlington, VA 22201
703/524-7600
www.nami.org

National Mental Health Association
2000 North Beauregard Street
6th Floor
Alexandria, VA 22311
800/969-6642
www.nmha.org

National Institute of Mental Health
6001 Executive Boulevard
Room 8148, MSC 9663
Bethesda, MD 20892-9663
866/615-6464
www.nimh.nih.gov

A

acupuncture, 80
adjustment disorder. *See* reactive depression.
adjustment strategies, 98
age, 15–16
alcohol abuse, 13, 31, 86, 87
American Psychological Association Web site, 46, 97
anger, 27, 32, 85, 102
animal-assisted therapy, 81
antidepressants. *See* medications.
appetite, 18–19, 27, 29, 88
autumn, 19

B

Beardslee, William, 48–49, 76, 86, 106
bipolar disorder, 17, 23, 44–45, 58, 71–72, 75, 77, 104
books, 97,106,
boredom, 30
boys. *See* males.
brain chemistry, 12, 40–43, 48, 71, 73
breakups, 7–8, 13, 53, 54, 62, 93
bullying, 21
bupropion, 77

C

Celexa, 77
Center for Mental Health Services, 10
chemical imbalance. *See* brain chemistry.
chronic depression, 55, 75
cigarettes, 31, 87
citalopram, 77
clinical depression, 10

cognitive-behavioral therapy (CBT). *See* psychotherapy.

concentration, 34, 95, 99
counselors, 57, 64, 97
Cymbalta, 77

D

death, 13, 17, 35
Depakote, 77
divalproex, 77
divorce, 17, 53
doctors. *See* physicians.
dopamine, 73, 104
drug abuse, 13, 86–87
drugs, 31, 49, 73, 74, 86–87, 102
duloxetine, 77
dysthymia, 17, 18

E

Effexor, 77
emotional abuse, 13
escitalopram, 77
exercise, 79, 94

F

Fassler, David, 10, 38,–39, 47, 50,–51, 62, 75, 83, 106
fatigue, 18, 19, 28
females, 16, 48
fluoxetine, 74, 76–77
friendship, 90, 100–101

G

gabapentin, 77
genetics, 12, 38–39, 43, 104
girls. *See* females.
Glass, Richard M., 76
group therapy, 62, 80
guilt, 27, 33

H

headaches, 27, 29
heredity. *See* genetics.
homelessness, 13
homework, 69
hopelessness, 26, 27, 33, 45, 60, 67, 85, 88
hormones, 41, 48, 73, 104

I

illnesses, 19
individualized education plans (IEPs), 99
insomnia, 37

K

"Katherine," 20–23, 26, 28–30, 35, 38–39, 44, 61, 70, 71, 83, 84, 94
"Kevin," 25, 26, 31, 34, 37, 38, 95, 100

L

"learned helplessness," 103
"learned optimism," 103
Lexapro, 77

M

magazines, 97
major depression, 15, 17–19,
males, 16, 48
manic-depressive disorder. *See* bipolar disorder.
medications. *See also* psychotherapy; treatments.
 antidepressants, 49, 72–73, 104
 chemical names, 77
 generic names, 77
 mood stabilizers, 23, 72
 psychotherapy and, 18, 57, 59, 61–63, 66, 68-69, 75, 92, 105
 selective serotonin reuptake inhibitors (SSRIs), 74, 105
meditation, 81
mental tune-ups. *See* psychotherapy.
mindfulness, 81
mood swings, 17, 23, 102

N

National Alliance on Mental Illness Web site, 97
National Institute of Mental Health Web site, 97
Nemours Foundation Web site, 97
neurons, 42, 74
Neurontin, 77
neuroreceptors, 42, 43
neurotransmitters, 12, 41, 42, 43, 73, 78, 79, 104
norepinephrine, 73, 105
nurse practitioners, 57

O

optimism, 103

P

Parkinson's disease, 19
paroxetine, 77
Paxil, 77
Pexeva, 77
phototherapy, 19, 79
physical abuse, 13
physical symptoms, 28–29
physicians, 57, 91, 97
poverty, 13
prejudice, 82
primary care physicians, 57
Prozac, 76, 77
psychiatrists, 57, 61, 75, 85, 105

psychologists, 23, 57, 60, 61, 71, 72, 97, 99, 103, 105, 112
psychotherapy. *See also* medications; treatment.
  cognitive-behavioral therapy (CBT), 51, 66–67, 76, 81
  definition of, 61, 105
  description of, 62–63
  homework, 69
  medications and, 23, 49, 59, 71–75, 77–78
  selecting, 53–54, 64–65
  mental tune-ups, 69
  therapeutic alliances, 68, 69
  therapeutic goals/contracts, 68
  therapy dogs, 63, 81
  types of therapists, 57, 85

Q

quiz, 51

R

reactive depression, 17, 18
recklessness, 31
referrals, 60
residential treatment centers, 99
restlessness, 27, 31, 37

S

sadness, 18, 21, 32, 45, 47, 85, 88
Saint-John's-wort (*Hypericum perforatum*), 78
"Samantha," 25, 26, 32, 33, 38, 96
Sarafem, 77
school counselors, 54, 60, 64, 85, 91, 101
Seasonal Affective Disorder (SAD), 17, 19, 79

selective serotonin reuptake inhibitors (SSRIs). *See* medications.
self-help groups. *See* group therapy.
self-medication. *See* alcohol abuse; drug abuse.
Seligman, Martin, 103
serotonin, 73, 74, 105
sertraline, 77
"Shannon," 6–9, 28, 29, 30, 52–54, 62, 82, 83, 85, 88, 93
signs, 10–11, 26, 27, 29, 31, 44, 46, 47, 50, 58, 84, 88–89
sleeping disorders, 8, 25-26, 28, 37
social workers, 54, 57, 61, 105
spring, 19
stigma, 82–83
stomachaches, 29
substance abuse. *See* alcohol abuse; drug abuse.
suicide, 35, 74, 88–89, 90, 91
Suicide Awareness Voices of Education, 76
summer, 19
support groups. *See* group therapy.
symptoms, 10–11, 18–20, 21, 23, 25–29, 32, 38, 43, 46, 47, 48, 50, 51, 59, 69, 76, 78, 84
synapses, 42, 43, 74

T

talk therapy, 57, 61, 105
therapeutic alliances. *See* psychotherapy.
therapeutic day schools, 99
therapeutic goals/contracts, 68
therapy. *See* psychotherapy.

therapy dogs. *See*
    psychotherapy.
thought patterns, 67
treatments. *See also* medication;
    psychotherapy.
  acupuncture, 80
  animal-assisted therapy, 81
  cognitive-behavioral therapy.
    See psychotherapy.
  exercise. *See* exercise.
  lack of, 35, 90
  major depression, 18
  mindfulness, 81
  phototherapy. *See*
    phototherapy.
  reactive depression, 18
  referrals, 60
  Seasonal Affective Disorder
    (SAD), 19
  self-help groups. *See* group
    therapy.
  statistics on, 55
  support groups. *See* group
    therapy.
triggers, 46, 50, 93–94

U
University of Vermont, 10

V
venlafaxine, 77

W
warning signs, 11
Web sites
  American Psychological
    Association, 97
  dot-com sites, 97
  National Alliance on Mental

    Illness, 97
  National Institute of Mental
    Health, 97
  Nemours Foundation, 97
  Suicide Awareness Voices of
    Education, 76
Wellbutrin, 77
winter, 17, 19, 79
worthlessness, 27, 33, 66, 67, 88

Z
Zoloft, 77

About the
Authors

Faye Zucker is a writer and editor who specializes in books about medicine, psychology, and education. She has a bachelors degree in linguistics and a masters in librarianship from the University of Chicago. Currently, Faye is working for Sage Publications in Thousand Oaks, California, as executive editor of Corwin Press, where she publishes books about teaching, learning, and school health.

Joan E. Huebl is a licensed clinical psychologist. She received her masters degree and doctorate from Pepperdine University's Graduate School of Education and Psychology. She also has bachelors and masters degrees in general studies in the humanities from the University of Chicago. Dr. Huebl is in private practice in northern Colorado. Her Web site is www.DrHuebl.com.

Acknowledgments
The authors thank Sherry Stone, Diane Tropper, and Paula Edelsack for their critical comments and insightful guidance during the development of this manuscript.